NATIONAL
SECURITY
STRATEGY
of the United States

Also available from Brassey's:

NATIONAL SECURITY STRATEGY OF THE UNITED STATES
by Ronald Reagan (1988)

An AUSA Book   An AFA Book

NATIONAL SECURITY STRATEGY

of the United States:
1990-1991

GEORGE BUSH

BRASSEY'S (US), Inc.

Maxwell Macmillan Pergamon Publishing Corp

WASHINGTON • NEW YORK • LONDON • OXFORD • BEIJING

FRANKFURT • SÃO PAULO • SYDNEY • TOKYO • TORONTO

First edition 1990

BRASSEY'S (US), INC.

Editorial Offices
Brassey's (US), Inc.
8000 Westpark Drive, 1st Floor
McLean, VA 22102

Order Department
Macmillan Publishing Co.
Front and Brown Streets
Riverside, NJ 08075

Brassey's (US), Inc., books are available at special discounts for bulk purchases for sales promotions, premiums, fund-raising, or educational use through the Special Sales Director, Macmillan Publishing Company, 866 Third Avenue, New York, New York 10022.

Library of Congress Cataloging-in-Publication Data

United States. President (1989–   : Bush)
    National security strategy of the United States,
1990–1991.

    (An AUSA book)
    "An AFA book."
    1. United States—National security. I. Bush,
George, 1924–   . II. Title. III. Series: Ausa
Institute of Land Warfare Book.
UA23.U4925   1990   355'.033073   90-1690
ISBN 0-08-036732-1

10   9   8   7   6   5   4   3   2   1

Publisher's Note

The *National Security Strategy of the United States* is the President's articulation to the U.S. Congress of American strategic objectives. Brassey's is pleased to publish this public document to ensure that it is broadly available to American citizens, who remain vitally interested in our nation's role in the world.

Senator John G. Tower
Chairman of the Board of Directors
Brassey's (US), Inc.

An AUSA Institute of Land Warfare Book

The Association of the United States Army, or AUSA, was founded in 1950 as a not-for-profit organization dedicated to education concerning the role of the U.S. Army, to providing material for military professional development, and to the promotion of proper recognition and appreciation of the profession of arms. Its constituencies include those who serve in the Army today, including Army National Guard, Army Reserve, and Army civilians, and the retirees and veterans who have served in the past, and all their families. A large number of public-minded citizens and business leaders are also an important constituency. The Association seeks to educate the public, elected and appointed officials, and leaders of defense industry on crucial issues involving the adequacy of our national defense, particularly those issues affecting land warfare.

In 1988 AUSA established within its existing

organization a new entity known as the Institute of Land Warfare. Its purpose is to extend the educational work of AUSA by sponsoring scholarly publications, to include books, monographs, and essays on key defense issues, as well as workshops and symposia. Among the volumes chosen for designation as "an AUSA Institute of Land Warfare Book" are both new texts and reprints of titles of enduring value that are no longer in print. Topics include history, policy issues, strategy, and tactics. Publication as an AUSA Book does not indicate that the Association of the United States Army and the publisher agree with everything in the book, but does suggest that the AUSA and the publisher believe this book will stimulate the thinking of AUSA members and others concerned about important issues.

An AFA /AEF Book

The Air Force Association (AFA), established on February 6, 1946, is an independent veterans' organization whose objective is to promote greater understanding of aerospace and national defense issues. On May 1, 1956, AFA established the Aerospace Education Foundation (AEF). The Foundation was established as a nonprofit organization in order to formulate and administer AFA's educational outreach programs.

With a membership of more than 240,000, AFA represents all elements of the Air Force family, military and civilian, active and retired, Reserve and National Guard, cadet and veteran, Civil Air Patrol, civil service, and aerospace workers.

Brassey's AFA Book Series is designed to assist AFA's Aerospace Education Foundation in fulfilling its mandate. AEF's goal is to inform AFA members—and indeed anyone involved in the national defense dialogue—about issues vital to the future of the U.S. Air Force in particular and air power in general. Forthcoming AFA Books may cover the topics of aerospace history, biography, technology, combat, strategy and tactics, personnel, management, leadership, and policy. Publication as "an AFA Book" does not indicate that the Air Force Association and the publisher agree with everything in the book, but does suggest that the AFA and the publisher believe this book will stimulate the thinking of AFA members and others concerned about important issues.

Contents

Preface

In the aftermath of World War II, the United States took on an unaccustomed burden—the responsibility to lead and help defend the world's free nations. This country took bold and unprecedented steps to aid the recovery of both allies and defeated foes, to provide a shield behind which democracy could flourish, and to extend its hand in aid of global economic progress. The challenge of an aggressive, repressive Soviet Union was contained by a system of alliances, which we helped create, and led.

In this historic endeavor, America has succeeded—brilliantly. But it was inevitable that new conditions created by this success would eventually call for a new kind of American leadership. It was inevitable that our overwhelming economic predominance after the war would be reduced as our friends, with our help, grew stronger. And perhaps it was inevitable that the Soviet Union, met by a strong coalition of free nations determined to resist its encroachments, would have to turn inward to face the internal contradictions of its own deeply flawed system— as our policy of containment always envisioned.

Today, after four decades, the international landscape is marked by change that is breathtaking in its character, dimension, and pace. The familiar moorings of postwar security policy are being loosened by developments that were barely imagined years or even months ago. Yet, our goals and interests remain constant. And, as we look toward—and hope for—a better tomorrow, we must also look to those elements of our past policy that have played a major role in bringing us to where we are today.

It is our steadfastness over four decades that has brought us to this moment of historic opportunity.

We will not let that opportunity pass, nor will we shrink from the challenges created by new conditions. Our response will require strategic vision—a clear perception of our goals, our interests, and the means available to achieve and protect them. The essence of strategy is determining priorities. We will make the hard choices.

This Report outlines the direction we will take to protect the legacy of the postwar era while enabling the United States to help shape a new era, one that moves beyond containment and that will take us into the next century.

I invite the American people and Congress to join us in a dialogue that will inform and enlighten the difficult decisions we will have to make in the months and years ahead.

March 1990

·I·

THE
FOUNDATIONS
OF NATIONAL
STRATEGY:
Goals and Interests

Enduring Elements of Our National Strategy

Throughout our history, our national security strategy has pursued broad, consistent goals. We have always sought to protect the safety of the nation, its citizens, and its way of life. We have also worked to advance the welfare of our people by contributing to an international environment of peace, freedom, and progress within which our democracy—and other free nations—can flourish.

These broad goals have guided American foreign and defense policy throughout the life of the Republic. They were as much the driving force behind President Jefferson's decision to send the American Navy against the Pasha of Tripoli in 1804 as they were when President Reagan directed American naval and air forces to return to that area in 1986. They animated Woodrow Wilson's Fourteen Points, and my initiatives in support of democracy in Eastern Europe this past year.

In addition, this Nation has always felt a pow-

erful sense of community with those other nations
that shared our values. We have always believed
that, although the flourishing of democracy in
America did not require a completely democratic
world, it could not long survive in one largely
totalitarian. It is a common moral vision that
holds together our alliances in Europe, East Asia,
and other parts of the world—a vision shaped by
the Magna Carta, our Declaration of Independence and Bill of Rights, the Declaration of the
Rights of Man, the United Nations Charter, the
Universal Declaration of Human Rights, and
the Helsinki Final Act. The American commitment to an alliance strategy, therefore, has a more
enduring basis than simply the perception of a
common enemy.

Another enduring element of our strategy has
been a commitment to a free and open international economic system. America has championed liberal trade to enhance world prosperity as
well as to reduce political friction among nations.
We must never forget the vicious cycle of protectionism that helped deepen the Great Depression and indirectly fostered the Second World

War. Like so many of its predecessors, my Administration is committed to working with all nations to promote the prosperity of the free market system and to reduce barriers that unfairly inhibit international commerce. In particular, it would be a tragedy of immense proportions if trade disputes weakened political ties that forty years of military threat could not undo.

Our location on the globe has also defined a consistent element of our security strategy. We have been blessed with large oceans east and west and friendly neighbors north and south. But many of our closest friends and allies and important economic and political interests are great distances from the United States. Therefore, in the modern era we have maintained the ability to project American power to help preserve the international equilibrium—globally and regionally—in support of peace and security.

In particular, for most of this century, the United States has deemed it a vital interest to prevent any hostile power or group of powers from dominating the Eurasian land mass. This interest remains. In the period since World War

II, it has required a commitment to forward defense and forward military deployments, and a recognition of the lesson of the 1930s—that peace and security come only through vigilance and preparedness. This strategy was described as a strategy of containment of Soviet expansionism. Its purpose was not the division of the world into American and Soviet spheres of influence, but, on the contrary, fostering the reemergence of independent centers of power in Europe and Asia. Behind this shield, our friends built up their strength and created institutions of unity (like the European Community), and our system demonstrated its political and economic vitality. It was our conviction that in these conditions, a steadfast policy of resistance to encroachments would, over time, in George Kennan's famous words, lead to "the breakup or the gradual mellowing of Soviet power."

This we now see. The very success of containment has created new conditions and new opportunities for a new generation of Americans. We welcome this change. Yet our basic values—

and our basic geopolitical necessities—remain. As the world's most powerful democracy, we are inescapably the leader, the connecting link in a global alliance of democracies. The pivotal responsibility for ensuring the stability of the international balance remains ours, even as its requirements change in a new era. As the world enters a period of new hope for peace, it would be foolhardy to neglect the basic conditions of security that are bringing it about.

Our Interests and Objectives in the 1990s

Our broad national interests and objectives are enduring. They can be summed up as follows:

The survival of the United States as a free and independent nation, with its fundamental values intact and its institutions and people secure.

The United States seeks, whenever possible in concert with its allies, to:

- deter any aggression that could threaten its security and, should deterrence fail, repel or defeat military attack and end conflict on terms favorable to the United States, its interests and allies;

- deal effectively with threats to the security of the United States and its citizens and interests short of armed conflict, including the threat of international terrorism;

- improve strategic stability by pursuing equitable and verifiable arms control agreements, modernizing our strategic deterrent, developing technologies for strategic defense, and strengthening our conventional capabilities;

- encourage greater recognition of the principles of human rights, market incentives, and free elections in the Soviet Union while fostering restraint in Soviet military spending and discouraging Soviet adventurism;

- prevent the transfer of militarily critical technologies and resources to hostile countries or groups, especially the spread of weapons of mass destruction and associated high-technology means of delivery; and

- reduce the flow of illegal drugs into the United States.

A healthy and growing U.S. economy to ensure opportunity for individual prosperity and a resource base for national endeavors at home and abroad.

National security and economic strength are indivisible. We seek to:

- promote a strong, prosperous, and competitive U.S. economy;

- ensure access to foreign markets, energy, mineral resources, the oceans, and space; and

- promote an open and expanding international economic system with minimal distortions to trade and investment, stable currencies, and broadly agreed and respected rules for managing and resolving economic disputes.

A stable and secure world, fostering political freedom, human rights, and democratic institutions.

We seek to:

- promote the rule of law and diplomatic solutions to regional conflicts;

- maintain stable regional military balances to deter those powers that might seek regional dominance;

- support aid, trade, and investment policies that promote economic development and social and political progress;

- promote the growth of free, democratic political institutions, as the surest guarantee of both human rights and economic and social progress; and

- aid in combatting threats to democratic institutions from aggression, coercion, insurgencies, subversion, terrorism, and illicit drug trafficking.

Healthy, cooperative and politically vigorous relations with allies and friendly nations.

To build and nurture such relationships, we seek to:

- strengthen and enlarge the commonwealth of free nations that share a commitment to democracy and individual rights;

- establish a more balanced partnership with our allies and a greater sharing of global leadership and responsibilities;

- support greater economic, political, and defense integration in Western Europe and a closer relationship between the United States and the European Community;

- work with our allies in the North Atlantic Alliance and fully utilize the processes of the Conference on Security and Cooperation in Europe to bring about reconciliation, security, and democracy in a Europe whole and free; and

- make international institutions more effective in promoting peace, world order, and political, economic and social progress.

·II·

TRENDS
IN THE
WORLD TODAY:
Opportunities
and Uncertainties

Broadly and properly understood, our national security strategy is shaped by the totality of the domestic and international environment—an environment that is today dramatically changing.

The Crisis in Communism

Future historians may well conclude that the most notable strategic development of the present period is the systemic crisis engulfing the Communist world. This crisis takes many forms and has many causes:

- After the Vietnam trauma of the 1970s, the West's political recovery in the 1980s—including its rearmament and such successes as the INF deployment in Europe—undermined the Soviet leaders' assumptions that the global "correlation of forces" was shifting in their favor.

- While the industrial democracies surge headlong into a post-industrial era of supercomputers, microelectronics, and telecommunications, Communist states have been mired in stagnation, paralyzed by outmoded statist dogmas that stifle innovation and productivity. Poor economic performance, especially in contrast with the West, has discredited a system that prided itself on its mastery of economic forces. And the new Information Revolution has posed for totalitarian regimes the particular challenge that clinging to old policies of restricting information would lead to permanent technological paralysis.

- A new Soviet leadership in the mid-1980s recognized that its system was in crisis and undertook an ambitious program of reform. Abroad, this leadership sought a calmer international environment in order to concentrate on its internal crisis. This has led, for example, to a Soviet troop withdrawal from Afghanistan and Soviet diplomatic interest in compromise solutions to regional conflicts, as Moscow sought gradually (and selectively) to scale back costly overseas commitments. These commitments had been made costly by indigenous resistance—supported by reinvigorated Western policies of engagement.

- In 1989, in parallel with the negotiation on Conventional Armed Forces in Europe (CFE), the Soviets began unilaterally reducing their heavy military burden and their presence in Eastern Europe, while proclaiming (and thus far demonstrating) a more tolerant policy toward their East bloc neighbors' internal affairs. We have seen powerful pent-up democratic forces unleashed all across Eastern Europe that have overturned Communist dictatorships and are reversing the pattern of Soviet dominance.

We are facing a strategic transformation born of the success of our postwar policies. Yet, such fundamental political change will likely be turbulent. There may be setbacks and new sources of instability. Happy endings are never guaranteed. We can only be impressed by the uncertainties that remain as the Soviet Union and the states of Eastern Europe, each in its own way, advance into historically uncharted waters.

The Industrial Democracies

The industrial democracies also face strategic challenges, some of them serious, but they too are largely the products of our success. These include a shifting balance of economic power and the danger that trade disputes in an era of economic change and adjustment could strain political and security ties. Such strains would be especially damaging at a moment when we need to maintain strength and unity to take best advantage of new opportunities in East-West relations which that strength and unity have helped bring about.

The growing strength and self-reliance of our

allies in Western Europe and East Asia have already resulted in a greater sharing of leadership responsibility—as the European Community (EC) has shown in policies towards Eastern Europe and as Japan has shown in international economic assistance.

One of the dramatic strategic developments of the 1990s will be the new role of Japan and Germany as successful democracies and economic and political leaders. U.S. policy has long encouraged such an evolution. It will provide powerful new reasons to maintain the partnerships— the Atlantic Alliance, the EC, and the U.S.-Japan security alliance—that have fostered reconciliation, reassurance, democracy, and security in Europe and Asia in the postwar period.

The Global Economy

In a new era of technological innovation and global markets, the world economy will be more competitive than ever before. The phenomenal growth in East Asia will likely continue, and by

early in the next century the combined output of
Japan, the Republic of Korea, China, and Taiwan
may exceed our own. Western Europe—as it progressively removes barriers to the free flow of
labor, capital, and goods within the EC—will become an even stronger economic power. The Soviet Union, even with a measure of success for
perestroika, will likely slip further behind the
United States, Japan, and Western Europe in output. In many other areas of the world, economic
expansion will not keep pace with population
growth or the debt burden, further squeezing resources and fomenting unrest and instability. All
these developments carry significant security im-
plications as well as their obvious economic and
social import.

The diffusion of economic power that will almost certainly continue is, in part, a reflection of
a wise and successful U.S. policy aimed at promoting worldwide economic growth. Provided
that the world economic system remains an open
and expanding one, we ourselves will benefit
from the growth of others. But American leadership will remain pivotal. A healthy American

economy is essential to sustain that leadership role, as well as to foster global economic development and ease dangerous pressures for unilateralism, regionalism, and protectionism.

Third World Conflicts

In a new era, some Third World conflicts may no longer take place against the backdrop of superpower competition. Yet many will, for a variety of reasons, continue to threaten U.S. interests. The erosion of U.S.-Soviet bipolarity could permit and in some ways encourage the growth of these challenges.

Highly destructive regional wars will remain a danger, made even greater by the expansion of the armed forces of regional powers and the proliferation of advanced weaponry. And it will be increasingly difficult to slow the spread of chemical, biological, and nuclear weapons—along with long-range delivery systems. Instability in areas troubled by poverty, injustice, racial, religious or ethnic tension will continue, whether or not exploited by the Soviets. Religious fanaticism may continue to endanger American lives, or countries friendly to us in the Middle East, on whose energy resources the free world continues to depend. The scourge of terrorism, and of states who sponsor it, likewise remains a threat.

Trends in Weaponry

Modern battlefields are characterized by an unprecedented lethality. The greater precision, range, and destructiveness of conventional weapons now extend war across a wider geographic area, and make it much more rapid and intense. As global weapons production becomes more diffused, these weapons are increasingly available to smaller powers, narrowing the military gap between ourselves and regional states and making some Third World battlefields in many ways as demanding as those we would expect in Central Europe.

The United States has a competitive edge in most technologies relevant to advanced weaponry, but we must continue to translate this advantage into fielded weapon systems supported by appropriate tactical doctrine and operational art. New conditions require continuing innovation as we move to incorporate stealth technology, extremely accurate weapons, improved means of locating targets, and new operational concepts into our combat forces.

Illicit Drugs

Traffic in illicit drugs imposes exceptional costs on the economy of the United States, undermines our national values and institutions, and is directly responsible for the destruction and loss of many American lives. The international traffic in illicit drugs constitutes a major threat to our national security and to the security of other nations.

We will increase our efforts to reduce both the supply of and the demand for illicit drugs. Internationally, we will attack the production of such drugs, and the multinational criminal organizations which enable illicit drugs to be processed, transported, and distributed. A cornerstone of our international drug control strategy is to work with and motivate other countries to help defeat the illicit drug trade and reduce the demand for drugs.

As we intensify our programs, we will increase our actions aimed at controlling the flow of drugs across our borders. In this area, as in others, we will make increased use of the resources and expertise provided by the Department of Defense. We recognize that military involvement in this mission has costs, and that in a world of finite resources increased effort here is at the expense of other important defense activities. We accept these trade-offs, and we will do the job.

Refugees

The dislocations of a turbulent world—famine, persecution, war, and tyranny—have swelled the wave of refugees across the planet to a total that now exceeds 14 million. Many have literally been forced from their homes by the heavy hand of tyranny.

Thousands of others have fled their homelands to escape oppression. Millions from Afghanistan, Ethiopia, and Mozambique have moved simply to stay alive. Others subsist in camps, from one generation to the next, awaiting solutions to seemingly intractable political and ethnic disputes. Beyond the deep personal tragedies these figures represent, such a vast refugee population taxes the world community's resources, denies to that community the many contributions these peoples could make in more benign circumstances, and fuels the hatreds that will ignite future conflicts.

The United States has a proud tradition, as long as our history, of welcoming refugees to our shores. We also take pride in our work with international agencies to provide assistance and relief for refugees, even as we strive politically to resolve the conflicts that provoked their flight. We have encouraged the restructuring of relief organizations to make them more effective and efficient—to make certain that scarce resources reach those who need them. This year, through our budget and the generosity of private groups, we will take in more refugees than last year. We will maintain a compassionate and generous program of resettlement in the United States and assistance for refugees worldwide.

Issues for the Future

The security environment we face in the 1990s is more hopeful, but in many ways also more uncertain than at any time in the recent past. Some of the questions before us are:

- How can we ensure continued international stability as U.S.-Soviet bipolarity gives way to global interdependence and multipolarity? What will be America's continuing leadership role—and the new roles of leadership assumed by our allies?

- What are the risks that today's positive strategic trends will be reversed, and how do we take due account of them in our long-term planning? How much risk can we prudently accept in an era of strategic change, fiscal austerity, and great uncertainty?

- While maintaining a balance of power with the Soviet Union as an inescapable American priority, how do we adapt our forces for the continuing challenge of contingencies elsewhere in the world?

- How do we maintain the cohesion among allies and friends that remains indispensable to common security and prosperity, as the perceived threat of a common danger weakens?

- What will be the structure of the new Europe—politically, economically, and militarily—as the Eastern countries move toward democracy and Germany moves toward unification?

- If military factors loom less large in a world of a more secure East-West balance,

how shall we marshall the other instruments of policy to promote our interests
and objectives?

In shaping a national security strategy for the
1990s, we will need answers to these and other
questions. Our preliminary assessments are re-
flected in the sections that follow.

·III·

REGIONAL CHALLENGES AND RESPONSES

Although we are a global power, our interests are not equally engaged or threatened everywhere. In the face of competing demands, budgetary stringency, and an improving East-West climate, we must review our priorities. Where our capabilities fall short of needs, we must assess the risks and employ the full panoply of our policy instruments to minimize them.

Our relationship with the Soviet Union retains a strategic priority because that country remains the only other military superpower. Even as tensions ease and military forces are reduced on both sides, maintaining the global strategic balance is inescapably an American concern; there is no substitute for our efforts.

Yet, the extraordinary changes taking place, if their promise is fulfilled, will permit important changes in our defense posture—*and* a greater possibility of viewing other regions in their own right, independent of the East-West context.

The Soviet Union

Our goal is to move beyond containment, to seek the integration of the Soviet Union into the international system as a constructive partner. For the first time in the postwar period, this goal appears within reach.

The Soviet Union has taken major steps toward rapprochement with the international system, after seventy years of seeking to undermine it; it has repudiated its doctrines of class warfare and military superiority and criticized major tenets of its own postwar policy. It has begun to move toward democracy. All this we can only applaud.

The United States will seek to engage the USSR in a relationship that is increasingly cooperative. Moscow will find us a willing partner in creating the conditions that will permit the Soviet Union to join, and be welcome in, a peaceful, free, and prosperous international community. We will expand contacts for mutual benefit, to promote the free flow of ideas and democratic values in the Soviet Union, and to lay a firmer foundation for a deeper relationship over the long term. Our Open Lands proposal, for example, would abolish the "closed zones" that unnecessarily impede contacts by diplomats, businessmen, tourists, students, and journalists. To support Soviet economic reform, I have proposed immediate negotiations on a U.S.-Soviet trade agreement so that—pending action by the Supreme Soviet to codify emigration reform—we could grant Most Favored Nation status to the Soviet Union at the June 1990 Summit. We have offered to support observer status for the Soviet Union in the structures created by the General Agreement on Tariffs and Trade (GATT) after the Uruguay Round of Multilateral Trade Negotiations is completed, and I personally urged Chairman Gorbachev to use the intervening time to move more rapidly towards market practices in the Soviet economy. We are also expanding technical economic cooperation and have begun discussions on a bilateral investment treaty.

We strongly support today's dramatic process of political and economic reform, and have a significant stake in its success. Yet, U.S. policy does not and cannot depend on a particular leader or set of leaders in the USSR. We look for fundamental alterations in Soviet institutions and practices that can only be reversed at great economic and political costs. In the political sphere, democracy is the best assurance of irreversible change. In the military sphere, with agreements in place—and weapons destroyed, production lines converted, and forces demobilized—any future Soviet leadership would find it costly, time-consuming, and difficult to renew the pursuit of military supremacy and impossible to attempt without providing ample strategic warning. These must be our standards.

Even if the U.S.-Soviet relationship remains competitive, it can be made less militarized and far safer. We will seek effectively verifiable arms control agreements with the Soviet Union and others as an integral component of our security strategy.

But whatever course the Soviets take over the next decade, the Soviet Union will remain a formidable military power. The United States must continue to maintain modern defenses that strengthen deterrence and enhance security. We cannot ignore continuing Soviet efforts to modernize qualitatively even as they cut back quantitatively. As Chairman Gorbachev declared last September 21st, "While reducing expenditure for [defense] purposes, we are paying attention to the qualitative rearmament of the Army, and in this way we are not permitting the overall level of our defense capability to be weakened in any degree." Our response thus represents prudent caution, but the Soviet leadership and people should realize that it is a caution based on uncertainty, not on hostility.

Restructuring the Soviet Union's relationship to the international community is as ambitious a task as containment was for its time. Responsibility for creating the conditions for it lies first and foremost with the Soviet Union itself. But the United States is determined, together with our allies, to challenge and test Soviet intentions and—while maintaining our guard—to work to put Soviet relations with the West on a firmer, more constructive course than had ever been thought possible in the postwar era.

Western Europe

The nations of the Atlantic Community, defined by their common values, are the founding members of a larger commonwealth of free nations—those states that share a commitment to freedom and individual rights. Ours is an alliance rooted in a shared history and heritage. Even if the military confrontation in Europe diminishes dramatically—as is our goal—the natural partnership of democratic allies will endure, grounded in its moral and political values.

The continued strength of the Alliance and our leadership within it remain essential to peace. The Soviet Union, even if its forces were pulled back entirely within its territory, would remain by virtue of geography a major military factor in Central Europe. Security and stability in Europe will therefore continue to depend on a substantial American presence, political and military. As I have repeatedly pledged, the United States will maintain significant military forces in Europe as long as our allies desire our presence as part of a common security effort. Our nuclear power remains the ultimate deterrent of aggression, even at lower force levels.

In Europe's emerging new political environment, moreover, the Atlantic Alliance remains a natural association of free nations and the natural framework for harmonizing Western policies on both security and diplomacy. It embodies the continuing American commitment to Europe; it also sustains the overall structure of stability that can assure the success of the democratic evolution of Central and Eastern Europe.

Yet, within this framework, the "European pillar" of the Atlantic world is being strengthened before our eyes—another dramatic development of this period. The United States categorically supports greater Western European economic and political integration, as a fulfillment of Europe's identity and destiny and as a necessary step toward a more balanced sharing of leadership and responsibility within the broader Atlantic Community. European unity and Alliance partnership do not conflict; they reinforce each other. We support the European Community's efforts to create a single unified market by 1992. A strong European Community will ensure more efficient use of European resources for common efforts, and will also be a strategic magnet to the nations of Eastern Europe. We also support increased Western European military cooperation and co-ordination, within the overall framework of the Atlantic Alliance, including both bilateral efforts and those in the Western European Union. We strongly support the independent British and French nuclear deterrent forces and their continued modernization.

The unification of Germany is coming about— by peaceful means, on the basis of democracy, and in the framework of the Western relationships that have nurtured peace and freedom for four decades. This is a triumph for the West. We expect a unified Germany to remain a member of both the North Atlantic Alliance and the European Community, as all of us seek to foster the conditions for wider reconciliation in Europe.

As the European-American relationship shifts, frictions can arise. Statesmanship will be needed to ease them. The challenges that the Western democracies face in this environment, however, are challenges to wise policy, not to the nature of their system. Assuming the democracies maintain discipline in their diplomatic, defense, and economic policies, we face an extraordinary opportunity to shape events in accordance with our values and our vision of the future.

Eastern Europe

The United States and its allies are dedicated to overcoming the division of Europe. All the countries of Eastern Europe are entitled to become part of the worldwide commonwealth of free nations as, one by one, they reclaim the European cultural and political tradition that is their heritage. Overcoming this division depends on their achievement of self-determination and independence. We will accept no arrangements with Moscow that would limit these rights, and we expect the Soviet Union to continue to repudiate in deeds as well as in words all right and pretext to intervene in the affairs of East European states.

A free and prosperous Eastern Europe is not a threat to legitimate Soviet security interests, and every day it becomes easier to envision the time when Eastern and Western states can freely associate in the same social and economic organizations. The Cold War began with the division of Europe. It can truly end only when Europe is whole again.

We share with our allies a vision of Europe whole and free:

- We believe democratic institutions and values will be the core of the new Europe, as it is these institutions and values that today stand vindicated.

- Even as fundamental political changes are still evolving, we place high priority on moving rapidly to a level of forces lower and more stabilizing, with greater openness for military activities.

The United States intends to play a role in fostering Eastern Europe's economic development, supporting its democratic institutions, and ensuring the overall structure of stability. It has become dramatically clear that the American role is welcomed by the peoples of Eastern Europe, who—in the new Europe that is emerging—see our presence as reassuring. Naturally, our relations with East European countries will be affected by their policies on matters of concern to us, such as espionage, illicit technology transfer, terrorism, and subversion in the Third World.

In November—as an investment in our own security as well as in the freedom and well-being of the peoples of Eastern Europe—I signed into law legislation authorizing $938 million in assistance to support democracy in Poland and Hungary. In my FY 1991 budget I have proposed an additional $300 million as we begin to expand our program to encompass other new East European democracies. In addition, we have offered our best advice and expertise in support of economic reform, trade liberalization, labor market reforms, private sector development, and environmental protection. This marks a major and positive step in bipartisan foreign policy and un-

derscores the strength of the American commitment to assist Eastern Europe's historic march
toward freedom.

We will also look to the Conference on Security
and Cooperation in Europe (CSCE) to play a
greater role, since the CSCE stands for the freedom of people to choose their destiny under a
rule of law with rulers who are democratically
accountable. We suggested last year that we expand the CSCE human rights basket to include
standards for democratic pluralism and free elections, and that we breathe new life into the economic dimension of CSCE by focusing on the
practical problems of the transition from stagnant
planned economies to free and competitive markets. The time is ripe for such steps.

The Western Hemisphere

The Western Hemisphere has within reach the
great goal of becoming history's first entirely
democratic hemisphere. The dramatic victory of
the Nicaraguan opposition in the February 25th

elections has given a significant boost to the underlying trend toward democracy evident in the region over the past several years. The United States has long considered that its own security is inextricably linked to the hemisphere's collective security, social peace, and economic progress. The resurgence of democracy supports these objectives, and strengthens our natural unity just as another traditional stimulus to solidarity—fear of an extra-hemispheric threat—is receding. In a new era, our hemispheric policy seeks a new spirit of mature partnership.

We must continue, however, to counter security threats. Improvement in our relations with Cuba depends upon political liberalization there and an end to its subversion of other governments and the undermining of the peace process in the region. In Nicaragua, our goal is to assist the new government of Violeta Chamorro in its efforts to nurture democratic institutions, rebuild the economy, and scale back the Nicaraguan military. We support the Salvadoran government's military and political efforts to defeat the Communist insurgency.

Central America remains a disruptive factor in the U.S.-Soviet relationship. We hold the Soviet Union accountable for the behavior of its clients, and believe that Soviet cooperation in fostering democracy in the region is an important test of the new thinking in Soviet policy.

We will find new ways to cooperate with our two closest neighbors, Canada and Mexico. We strongly support the new democratic government in Panama, which is also the best long-term guarantee of the security and efficient operation of the Panama Canal. We will continue to seek a transition to democracy in Haiti, promoting international efforts in support of free elections. The return to democracy in most of Latin America will put new emphasis on our efforts to support professional, apolitical militaries. We will also confront the challenge to democracy posed by the drug trade and debt problems.

East Asia and the Pacific

Our network of alliances and our forces deployed in the region have ensured the stability that has made this area's striking progress possible.

In addition to our own deterrent strength, security in the region has rested since the 1970s on an unprecedented structure of harmonious relations among the region's key states. Our alliance with Japan remains a centerpiece of our security policy and an important anchor of stability. Japan's importance is now global. Our relationship is one of the most important bilateral relationships in the world and it is in our strategic interest to preserve it.

The relationship between the United States and China, restored in the early 1970s after so many years of estrangement, has also contributed crucially to regional stability and the global balance of power. The United States strongly deplored the repression in China last June and we have imposed sanctions to demonstrate our displeasure. At the same time, we have sought to avoid a total cutoff of China's ties to the outside world. Those ties not only have strategic importance, both globally and regionally; they are crucial to China's prospects for regaining the path of economic reform and political liberalization. China's angry isolation would harm all of these prospects.

The U.S. security commitment to the Republic of Korea remains firm; we seek a reduction in tensions on the Korean peninsula and fully endorse Seoul's efforts to open a fruitful South-North dialogue. Our strong and healthy ties with our ally Australia contribute directly to regional and global stability. The Association of Southeast Asian Nations (ASEAN) continues to play a major role in the region's security and prosperity.

In Cambodia, the United States seeks a comprehensive settlement, one which will bring the Cambodian people true peace and a government they have freely chosen.

As we have amply demonstrated, we support the Philippines' democratic institutions and its efforts to achieve prosperity, social progress, and internal security. We will negotiate with the Philippines in good faith on the status of our military facilities there. These facilities support a continued and needed American forward presence that benefits us, the Philippines, regional security, and global stability.

The Middle East and South Asia

The free world's reliance on energy supplies from this pivotal region and our strong ties with many of the region's countries continue to constitute important interests of the United States.

Soviet policies in the region show signs of moderating, but remain contradictory. The supply of advanced arms to Libya and Syria continues (as does the cultivation of Iran), though Soviet diplomacy has moved in other respects in more constructive directions.

The Middle East is a vivid example, however, of a region in which, even as East-West tensions diminish, American strategic concerns remain. Threats to our interests—including the security of Israel and moderate Arab states as well as the free flow of oil—come from a variety of sources. In the 1980s, our military engagements—in Lebanon in 1983–84, Libya in 1986, and the Persian Gulf in 1987–88—were in response to threats to U.S. interests that could not be laid at the Kremlin's door. The necessity to defend our interests will continue.

Therefore, we will maintain a naval presence in the eastern Mediterranean Sea, the Persian Gulf, and the Indian Ocean. We will conduct periodic exercises and pursue improved host-nation support and prepositioning of equipment throughout the region. In addition, we will discourage destabilizing arms sales to regional states, especially where there is the potential for upsetting local balances of power or accelerating wasteful arms races. We are especially committed to working to curb the proliferation of nuclear, chemical, and other weapons of mass destruction, the means to produce them, and associated long-range delivery systems. We will confront and build international pressure against those states that sponsor terrorism and subversion. And we will continue to promote a peace process designed to satisfy legitimate Palestinian political rights in a manner consonant with our enduring commitment to Israel's security.

In South Asia, Pakistan and India are both friends of the United States. We applaud the return of democracy to Pakistan and the trends of economic liberalization in both countries. We will seek to maintain our special relationship with our traditional ally Pakistan, steadily improve our relations with India, and encourage Indo-Pakistani rapprochement and a halt to nuclear proliferation. While we welcome the withdrawal of Soviet military forces from Afghanistan, the massive and continuing Soviet arms supply to the illegitimate regime in Kabul reinforces the need for continued U.S. support to the Mujahiddin in their quest for self-determination for the Afghan people. We remain firmly committed to a comprehensive political settlement as the best means of achieving Afghan self-determination and regional security.

Africa

Institution-building, economic development, and
regional peace are the goals of our policy in Africa. The global trends of democracy must come
to Africa too. All these goals must be achieved if
Africa is to play its rightful role as an important
factor in the international system. Africa is a major contributor to the world supply of raw ma-
terials and minerals and a region of enormous
human potential.

In the strategic dimension, the United States
has pressed hard throughout the 1980s for the
liquidation of all the Soviet/Cuban military in-
terventions in Africa left over from the 1970s.
The New York Accords of December, 1988,
were the culmination of an eight-year U.S. effort
for peace in Angola, and independence for Namibia. As a result, Cuban forces are departing
Angola, and Namibia will become independent
on March 21st. In the Horn of Africa, the United
States has encouraged negotiated solutions to the
region's conflicts.

In the economic dimension, the United States will continue to advocate reforms that eliminate wasteful and unproductive state-owned enterprises and that liberate the productive private sector and individual initiative. The United States has significantly increased the assistance it provides through our Development Fund for Africa. We continue to be the biggest donor of humanitarian aid and have helped international organizations and voluntary associations to distribute food, medicines, and other assistance.

We continue to press for a rapid and complete end to South Africa's system of apartheid. We support negotiations leading to a democratic, non-racial South Africa that would enhance long-term stability in the country and the region. We are encouraged by the progress that has been made, particularly the release of Nelson Mandela and the unbanning of political organizations. We look to all parties to continue to take the steps necessary to create a climate in which productive negotiations can take place.

·IV·

RELATING MEANS
TO ENDS:
Our Political
Agenda

The elements of our national power—diplomatic and political, economic and military—remain formidable. Yet, the relative importance of these different instruments of policy will change in changing circumstances. Our most difficult decisions will include not only which military forces or programs to adjust, increase, reduce or eliminate, but also which risks can be ameliorated by means other than military capability—means like negotiations, burdensharing, economic and security assistance, economic leverage, and political leadership.

In a new era, we foresee that our military power will remain an essential underpinning of the global balance, but less prominently and in different ways. We see that the more likely demands for the use of our military forces may not involve the Soviet Union and may be in the Third World, where new capabilities and approaches may be required. We see that we must look to our economic well-being as the foundation of our long-term strength. And we can see that, especially in the new international environment, political will and effective diplomacy can be what translates national power into the achievement of national objectives. While this Report necessarily describes these different elements of policy separately, national strategy must integrate them and wield them according to a coherent vision.

Alliance Relationships

Our first priority in foreign policy remains solidarity with our allies and friends. We have never been able to "go it alone", even in the early days of the Cold War when our major allies were still suffering from the devastation and exhaustion of World War II. Even to attempt to do so would alter our way of life and national institutions and would jeopardize the very values we are seeking to protect.

The rise of other centers of power in the free world is therefore welcome, consistent with America's values, and supportive of our national interests. We must ensure that free nations continue to recognize the fundamental moral, political, and security interests we have in common and protect those interests against both the residual threat of Soviet military power and the emerging threats of regional conflict and of divisive economic issues. We are prepared to share more fully with our allies and friends the responsibilities of global leadership.

Arms Control

Arms control is a means, not an end; it is an important component of a broader policy to enhance national security. We will judge arms control agreements according to several fundamental criteria:

- First, agreements must add to our security. Our objective is to reduce the incentives, even in crisis, to initiate an attack. Thus, we seek not reductions for reductions' sake, but agreements that will promote stability. We will work to reduce the capabilities most suited for offensive action or preemptive strike.

- Second, to enhance stability, we favor agreements that lead to greater predictability in the size, nature, and evolution of military forces. Predictability through openness expands the traditional focus of arms control beyond just military capabilities and addresses the fear of aggressive intent.

- Third, agreements are effective only if we can verify compliance. As we broaden our agenda to include issues like chemical and missile proliferation, verification will become an increasingly difficult challenge, but effective verification will still be required. We want agreements that can endure.

- Finally, since the security of the United States is indivisible from that of its friends and allies, we will insist that any arms control agreements not compromise allied security.

The arms control accomplishments of the past twelve months are impressive. We have already reached a number of new agreements with the Soviet Union on:

- prevention of dangerous military activities;

- advance notification of strategic exercises;

- clarification of the rights of innocent passage in territorial seas;

- a memorandum of understanding implementing verification provisions of the INF Treaty;

- trial verification and stability measures for Strategic Arms Reduction Talks (START);

- reciprocal demonstrations of each side's proposed procedures for verifying re-entry vehicles on ballistic missiles;

- reciprocal exhibitions of strategic bombers to aid verification; and

   • demonstrations of proposed "unique iden-
     tifiers" or "tags" for ballistic-missile verifi-
     cation.

   These are but the beginning. Our arms control
agenda is now broader than ever—beyond the
traditional East-West focus on nuclear weapons.
We are dealing with pressing multilateral arms
control issues. We are also negotiating for greater
transparency and for limits on conventional arms.
We will negotiate in good faith, patiently and
seriously, but we will not seek agreement for
agreement's sake, nor compromise the basic principles set forth above.

Strategic Arms Reduction Talks (START)

   In START, our goals are not merely to reduce
forces but to reduce the risk of nuclear war and
create a more stable nuclear balance. Our pro-

posals are designed to strengthen deterrence by reducing and constraining in particular those strategic nuclear forces which pose the greatest threat—namely, ballistic missiles, especially large ICBMs with multiple warheads. We propose less strict limits on bombers and cruise missiles, which are not capable of carrying out a disarming first strike. Our goal is to resolve all substantive START issues by the June 1990 Summit.

Defense and Space

Our approach to this set of issues, as well, is to enhance strategic stability by facilitating a cooperative transition to a stable balance of offensive and defensive forces if effective defenses prove feasible. We also seek greater transparency and predictability in approaches to strategic defense, and have proposed regular exchanges of data, briefings, visits to laboratories, and observations of tests.

Conventional Armed Forces in Europe (CFE)

The United States is firmly committed to reaching an agreement to reduce conventional armed forces in Europe to lower levels in order to enhance security and stability and to reduce the ability to launch a surprise attack or sustain large-scale offensive operations. Our goal is to complete the CFE Treaty as soon as possible this year. In my State of the Union speech, in response to rapid changes in Europe, I proposed to lower substantially the levels of U.S. and Soviet ground and air force personnel in Central and Eastern Europe—to 195,000 troops. This proposal has been accepted.

Chemical Weapons

The Conference on Disarmament in Geneva continues to work toward a global ban of chemical weapons, using as the basis for its negotiations the draft text that I personally presented for the

United States in 1984. It is one of my most important goals to see an effective, truly global ban of chemical weapons—their production and possession, as well as their use. At the United Nations and at Malta, I made several suggestions and challenges to speed this negotiation to a successful conclusion, including ways that the United States and Soviet Union can set an example to spur achievement of a global ban. In this connection, we and the Soviets have agreed to work together to sign a bilateral agreement at the June 1990 Summit that would have each side destroy substantial quantities of its chemical weapons stocks. We must not only deal with those states that now possess chemical weapons, but also address the growing proliferation of these instruments of indiscriminate destruction.

Open Skies

An important step in achieving predictability through openness is the Open Skies initiative I made last May, which would allow frequent unarmed observation flights over the territory of participating states. This would institutionalize openness on a truly unprecedented scale. It would achieve greater transparency about military activities, lessen danger, and ease tension. The NATO allies agreed in December on a common approach for pursuing this initiative, and foreign ministers from NATO and the Warsaw Pact have met in Ottawa to begin negotiating an agreement.

Confidence- and Security-Building Measures

These negotiations in Vienna are another important opportunity to enhance free world security through a variety of measures to codify openness and transparency in military operations and force structures. The recently completed seminar on military doctrine is a powerful example of how this forum can generate valuable exchanges among high-ranking military officers and open up new avenues of understanding.

Nuclear Testing

The United States and the Soviet Union are on the verge of completing new verification protocols to the 1974 Threshold Test Ban and the 1976 Peaceful Nuclear Explosions Treaties that should open the way to their ratification and entry into force. The protocols—which I expect to be signed at the June 1990 Summit—involve new, complex, and unprecedented techniques for effective verification, including direct, on-site measurement of explosive yield.

Proliferation

The spread of ever more sophisticated weaponry—including chemical, biological, and nuclear weapons—and of the missiles capable of carrying them represents a growing danger to international security. This proliferation exacerbates and fuels regional tensions and complicates U.S. defense planning. It poses ever greater dangers to U.S. forces and facilities abroad, and possibly even to the United States itself.

Our comprehensive approach to this problem includes stringent controls and multilateral co-operation designed to stop the spread of these technologies and components. We will work to strengthen the International Atomic Energy Agency, the Nuclear Non-Proliferation Treaty, and the Missile Technology Control Regime. We will also use diplomacy and economic and security assistance to address the underlying causes of tension or insecurity that lead countries to seek advanced weaponry.

Naval Forces

The Soviet Union has urged that we negotiate limitations on naval forces. We have rejected this proposal for reasons grounded in the fundamental realities of the free world's strategic interests.

The economies of the United States and its major allies depend so vitally on trade, and on the security of sea lines of communication, that we have always defined a vital interest in freedom of the seas for all nations. Our Navy protects that interest. Similarly, some of our most important security relations are with nations across the oceans. The Soviet Union, as a power on the Eurasian land mass not dependent on overseas trade, with interior lines of communication to its major allies and trading partners, has no such strategic stake. Its navy has served the purposes of coastal defense— or of denial of our ability to defend our vital interests. There is no symmetry here.

Nor is our naval power to be equated with the Soviet ground-force superiority that we are determined to reduce—a superiority that in its very nature, scope, and composition has posed an offensive threat. No navy could pose such a threat to the Soviet Union.

The Contest of Ideas and the Nurturing of Democracy

Since the end of World War II, the United States has developed and maintained an extensive program of public information around the world— through U.S. Information Agency offices at our embassies, speakers, publications, exchange programs, cultural centers, and numerous other activities.

A special effort has been made to reach into closed societies with information about their countries, factual news of the world, and insight into American society. Primary tools for this effort are the Voice of America, Radio Liberty, and Radio Free Europe. Their impact has been invaluable, and has contributed significantly to the changes now taking place in the Soviet Union, Eastern Europe, and elsewhere.

The American message of democracy, respect for human rights, and the free flow of ideas is as crucial and inspiring today as it was forty-five years ago. The truth we provide remains a stimulus to openness. In the coming decade, we will have to project American values and protect American interests on issues of growing global importance, such as the battle against narcotics trafficking and the search for solutions to international environmental problems.

An American intitiative begun in the 1980s—the National Endowment for Democracy—has broken new ground, mobilizing the private efforts of our political parties, labor unions, businesses, educational and other organizations in fostering the development of democratic institutions. As democratic change continues around the world— and is still denied in many places—we must ensure that the message we send and the means of delivery we use keep pace.

Economic and Security Assistance

Our foreign assistance has traditionally supported our security objectives by strengthening allies and friends, bolstering regional security, deterring conflict, and securing base rights and access.

As East-West tensions diminish, these political and economic instruments become more centrally relevant to an era of new challenges:

- A multipolar world, in which military factors may recede to the background, puts a new premium on the instrumentalities of political relations—of which foreign assistance has been one of the most cost-effective and valuable.

- In a new era, nurturing democracy and stability remains a basic goal, but one now freed from its traditional Cold War context. Foreign assistance is an indispensable means toward this end.

- Economic and humanitarian goals—such as promoting market-oriented structural reforms in Eastern Europe and the developing world, or aiding refugees and disaster victims—will also loom larger than before. This is a responsibility we need to share with international financial institutions and prosperous allies, but we need to do our part.

- As regional conflicts are resolved, United Nations peacekeeping takes on additional tasks—and will have a claim on our support. As for those conflicts that continue to fester, security assistance can reduce the

> level or likelihood of a direct U.S. role in
> bolstering regional security.

- On problems such as drugs, the environment, terrorism, or the proliferation of
  high-tech weaponry, U.S. aid remains a
  valuable tool of policy.

These policy instruments in our International
Affairs budget have always struggled for survival
in the congressional budget process. Low funding
and excessive earmarking and conditionality have
hampered flexibility. In the 1990s, we will need
to do justice to the growing needs of the emerging
East European democracies without validating
the fears of our Third World friends that they
will be relegated to second place. A national security strategy that takes us beyond containment
needs these tools more than ever.

Military Openness

In addition to the confidence-building measures discussed above, our policy seeks other ways of changing East-West military relations toward our goal of greater transparency. A prudent program of military-to-military contacts can demonstrate the capabilities of our forces while allowing us greater access to and understanding of the military establishments of potential adversaries. This can reduce worst-case planning based on limited information and reduce the likelihood of miscalculation or dangerous military incidents.

As the Soviet political system evolves, we hope that Soviet military power will increasingly be subject to detailed and searching public debate. In the long term, a Soviet military that must justify its size, mission, and resource demands to the Soviet public and legislature will find it more difficult to enhance its capabilities beyond the legitimate needs of defense. Increased contact with the armed forces of the United States and other democracies can aid this process as well as contribute to greater understanding. We will continue to pursue the kinds of contacts first agreed to by Admiral Crowe and Marshal Akhromeyev in 1988. We will also pursue similar exchanges with the armed forces of Eastern European states. In addition to their obvious contributions to transparency, such contacts will support our overall approach to Eastern Europe by helping the military officers of these states establish a professional identity independent of their roles in the Warsaw Pact.

·V·

RELATING MEANS
TO ENDS:
Our Economic
Agenda

America's national power continues to rest on the strength and resilience of our economy. To retain a position of international leadership, we need not only skilled diplomacy and strong military forces, but also a dynamic economic base with competitive agricultural and manufacturing sectors, an innovative research establishment, solid infrastructure, secure supplies of energy, and vibrant financial and service industries.

We will pursue a strategy that integrates domestic economic policies with a market-opening trade policy, enhanced cooperation among the major industrial countries, and imaginative solutions to the problems of the Third World.

Global Imbalances

Japan and Germany continue to run substantial trade and current account surpluses; the United States has large deficits. Recent economic summits and meetings of finance ministers of the

Group of Seven (G-7) have given high priority
to reducing these imbalances. For deficit countries like the United States, this requires action
to reduce budget deficits and encourage private
savings. The surplus countries like Germany and
Japan should, for their part, pursue macroeconomic policies and structural reforms to encourage non-inflationary growth. Through the
G-7 and economic summits, we will strengthen
coordination and ensure implementation of appropriate policies for non-inflationary growth and
expanded trade.

Debt

Aggregate Third World debt is over $1 trillion,
and debtor nations need some $70 billion just to
meet annual interest payments. It is a tremendous
burden on struggling democracies and on the ability of many friendly countries to maintain their
security. Relatively slow world growth, growing
inflation, rising unemployment, and the failure
to implement necessary economic reforms aggra-

vate an already difficult situation. We have advanced, in the Brady Plan, suggestions to revitalize the international debt strategy through reductions in commercial bank debt and debt service payments, as a complement to new lending. The International Monetary Fund and the World Bank will provide financial support for these efforts. As an essential first step in obtaining this support, we are urging debtors to adopt medium-term economic programs—including measures to strengthen domestic savings, steps to attract foreign investment, and policies that promote the return of flight capital.

Trade

Support within the United States for free trade has weakened as a result of persistently high trade deficits. Additional concern about the competitiveness of the U.S. economy has led to increased calls for government intervention in support of key sectors. Current account and trade deficits are macroeconomic phenomena that primarily re-

flect domestic savings and investment. The im-
balance between the U.S. saving rate and the
higher U.S. investment rate is, therefore, the
fundamental source of the U.S. trade deficit.
The net capital inflow into the United States,
which is necessary to finance the deficit, must
be matched by a corresponding increase in im-
ports to the United States, over exports to other
countries. The key to reducing the deficit, therefore, is to increase domestic saving, thus closing
the savings-investment gap and reducing import demand. We have proposed a comprehensive Savings and Economic Growth Act to raise
household savings which will help to restore
necessary balance in the trade and current ac-
counts.

While addressing the domestic causes for the
trade deficit, we must also ensure that market
forces are free to operate at home and abroad,
and that trade expands—rather than closing our
markets. In this regard, we will work with other
members of GATT to bring to a successful conclusion this year the Uruguay Round of Multi-

lateral Trade Negotiations now addressing issues crucial to our interests, including agricultural subsidies, services, the protection of intellectual property, trade-related investment measures, and market access. These are the trade problems of the 1990s that require solution if we are to maintain a domestic consensus in support of free and open trade.

Given the continuing strategic importance of unity among the industrial democracies, it is essential that trade disputes be resolved equitably, without tearing the fabric of vital political and security partnerships.

Technology

Our economic and military strength rests on our technological superiority, not sheer manufacturing might. The United States remains in the forefront in the development of new technologies, but American enterprises must respond more quickly in their exploitation of new technologies if they are to maintain their competitiveness in both domestic and foreign markets. The loss of advanced production capabilities in key industries could place our manufacturing base in jeopardy.

The dynamics of the technological revolution transcend national boundaries. The transfer of technology between allies and friends has benefitted the United States in both national security and economic terms. Open markets and open investment policies will best ensure that scarce resources are used efficiently and that benefits are widely shared. But the openness of the free market economy must not be exploited to threaten our security. With our partners in the Coordinating Committee for Multilateral Export Controls (COCOM), we must continue to work to ensure that militarily sensitive technology does not flow to potential adversaries. At the same time, we must adapt the procedures and lists of COCOM-controlled goods to support rapid political and economic change in Eastern Europe. In that regard, our task is threefold: (a) streamline COCOM controls on strategic goods and technologies; (b) harmonize and tighten national licensing and enforcement procedures; and (c) encourage greater cooperation with non-COCOM developing countries. We have also initiated a comprehensive analysis of the changing strategic threat, which will be instrumental in deciding on possible further changes in the multilateral system of strategic export controls.

Energy

Secure supplies of energy are essential to our prosperity and security. The concentration of 65 percent of the world's known oil reserves in the Persian Gulf means we must continue to ensure reliable access to competitively priced oil and a prompt, adequate response to any major oil supply disruption. We must maintain our Strategic Petroleum Reserve at a level adequate to protect our economy against a serious supply disruption. We will continue to promote energy conservation and diversification of oil and gas sources, while expanding our total supply of energy to meet the needs of a growing economy. We must intensify efforts to promote alternative sources of energy (nuclear, natural gas, coal, and renewables), and devote greater attention to reducing fossil fuel emissions in light of growing environmental concerns.

·VI·

RELATING MEANS TO ENDS:
Our Defense Agenda

One reason for the success of America's grand strategy of containment has been its consistency. The military component of that strategy has been adjusted to changing threats and available military technology, but there too substantial continuity remains:

- *Deterrence:* Throughout the postwar period we have deterred aggression and coercion against the United States and its allies by persuading potential adversaries that the costs of aggression, either nuclear or conventional, would exceed any possible gain. "Flexible response" demands that we preserve options for direct defense, the threat of escalation, and the threat of retaliation.

- *Strong Alliances:* Shared values and common security interests form the basis of our system of collective security. Collective defense arrangements allow us to combine our economic and military strength, thus lessening the burden on any one country.

- *Forward Defense:* In the postwar era, the defense of these shared values and common interests has required the forward presence of significant American military forces in Europe, in Asia and the Pacific, and at sea. These forces provide the capability, with our allies, for early, direct defense against aggression and serve as a visible reminder of our commitment to the common effort.

- *Force Projection:* Because we have global security interests, we have maintained ready forces in the United States and the means to move them to reinforce our units forward deployed or to project power into areas where we have no permanent presence. For the threat of protracted conflict we have relied on the potential to mobilize the manpower and industrial resources of the country.

These elements have been underwritten by advanced weaponry, timely intelligence, effective and verifiable arms control, highly qualified and trained personnel, and a system for command and control that is effective, survivable, and enduring. Together they have formed the essence of our defense policy and military strategy during the postwar era.

The rebuilding of America's military strength during the past decade was an essential underpinning to the positive change we now see in the international environment. Our challenge now is to adapt this strength to a grand strategy that looks beyond containment, and to ensure that our military power, and that of our allies and friends, is appropriate to the new and more complex opportunities and challenges before us.

Overall Priorities

From the weapons, forces, and technologies that will be available, we will have to pick carefully those that best meet our needs and support our strategy in a new period. Our approach will include the following elements:

- Deterrence of nuclear attack remains the cornerstone of U.S. national security. Regardless of improved U.S.-Soviet relations and potential arms control agreements, the Soviets' physical ability to initiate strategic nuclear warfare against the United States will persist and a crisis or political change in the Soviet Union could occur faster than we could rebuild neglected strategic forces. A START agreement will allow us to adjust how we respond to the requirements of deterrence, but tending to those requirements remains the first priority of our defense strategy.

- As we and our allies adjust our military posture, each should emphasize retaining those roles it is uniquely or better able to fulfill. For the United States, these include nuclear and space forces, advanced technologies, strategic mobility, a worldwide presence, power projection, and a secure mobilization base.

- As a country separated from many of its allies and areas of interest by vast distances, we will ensure we have those forces needed to control critical sea and air lines of communication in crisis and war.

- U.S. technological superiority has long been a powerful contributor to deterrence. To retain this edge, we will sustain our investment in research and development as an important hedge against an uncertain future.

- We remain committed to the doctrine of competitive strategies. I reaffirm the wisdom of exploiting American strengths in a systematic way, moving Soviet investment into areas that threaten us less or negating systems that threaten us most.

- Defense investment faces a dual challenge: to maintain sufficient forces to deter gen-

eral war while also giving us forces that
are well suited for the more likely contingencies of the Third World. Many defense
programs contribute significantly in both
environments but, where necessary, we
will develop the weaponry and force structure needed for the special demands of the
Third World even if it means that some
forces are less optimal for a conflict on the
European central front.

- As we make fundamental changes in our
  military forces, we will preserve a capacity
  for reversibility. This will affect decisions
  on a variety of issues and may, in the short
  run, reduce the amount of savings we
  might otherwise see. But it is a prudent
  hedge against future uncertainty, which it
  is my moral and constitutional duty to
  provide.

Deterring Nuclear War

Strategic Offensive Forces

The Soviet Union continues to modernize its strategic forces across the board. Even as START promises to reduce numbers substantially, the qualitative competition has not ended.

Decisions on strategic modernization that I have already made take advantage of the most promising technologies in each leg of our Triad to increase stability. The B-2 bomber will ensure our ability to penetrate Soviet defenses and fulfill the role the bomber force has played so successfully for forty years. The D-5 missile in Trident submarines will exploit the traditionally high survivability of this leg and add a significant ability to attack more hardened targets. In a two-phase program for our ICBM force, the deployment of the Rail Garrison System will enhance stability by removing Peacekeeper missiles from vulnerable silos and providing the mobile capability we need for the near term. In the second phase, deployment of the small ICBM road-mobile system will further strengthen stability and increase force flexibility.

While we will ensure that each leg of the Triad is as survivable as possible, the existence of all three precludes the destruction of more than one by surprise attack and guards against a technological surprise that could undermine a single leg.

Strategic Defenses

Flexible response and deterrence through the threat of retaliation have preserved the security of the United States and its allies for decades. Looking to the future, the Strategic Defense Initiative offers an opportunity to shift deterrence to a safer and more stable basis through greater reliance on strategic defenses. In a new international environment, as ballistic-missile capabilities proliferate, defense against third-country threats also becomes an increasingly important benefit.

The deterrent value of strategic defenses derives from the effect they would have on an adversary's calculations. Even an initial deployment would influence an attacker's calculation by diminishing his confidence in his ability to execute an effective attack. Initial strategic defenses would also offer the United States and its allies some protection should deterrence fail or in the event of an accidental launch. Follow-on deployments incorporating more advanced technologies could provide progressively more capable defenses, even in the face of countermeasures.

We continue to seek with the Soviet Union a cooperative transition to deployed defenses and reductions in strategic offensive arms. Strategic defenses can protect our security against possible violations of agreements to reduce strategic offensive weapons.

The Soviets have stated that they are no longer making completion and implementation of a START treaty contingent on a Defense and Space Agreement restricting SDI. A START Treaty should stand on its own merits and we will preserve our right to conduct SDI activities consistent with the Anti-Ballistic Missile (ABM) Treaty and our option to deploy SDI when it is ready. And we will use the Defense and Space Talks to explore a cooperative and stable transition to a greater reliance on stability-enhancing, cost-effective strategic defenses.

Theater Nuclear Forces

The Atlantic Alliance has consistently followed the principle of maintaining survivable and credible theater nuclear forces to ensure a robust deterrent, to execute its agreed strategy of flexible response—and to "couple" European defense to the strategic nuclear guarantee of the United States. At the same time, we have always pursued a nuclear force that is as small as is consistent with its tasks and objectives. Indeed, NATO has unilaterally reduced its theater nuclear weapons by over one-third during the past decade—over and above the entire class of U.S. and Soviet nuclear weapons eliminated by the INF Treaty. As requirements change, we will continue to ensure that our posture provides survivability and credibility at the lowest possible levels. The United States believes that for the foreseeable future, even in a new environment of reduced conventional forces and changes in Eastern Europe, we will need to retain modern nuclear forces in-theater.

Command, Control and Communications

Another basic element of deterrence is the security of our command and control, enhancing the certainty of retaliation. In addition, we maintain programs to ensure the continuity of constitutional government—another way of convincing a potential attacker that any attempted "decapitating" strike against our political and military leadership will fail.

Deterring Conventional War

It is clear that the United States must retain the full range of conventional military capabilities, appropriately balanced among combat and sup-

port elements, U.S.- and forward-based forces,
active and reserve components. We must also
maintain properly equipped and well trained general purpose and special operations forces. Within
these requirements, as we look to the future, we
see our active forces being smaller, more global
in their orientation, and having a degree of agility,
readiness and sustainability appropriate to the demands of likely conflicts.

Forward Defense through
Forward Presence

American leadership in the postwar world and
our commitment to the forward defense of our
interests and those of our allies have been underwritten by the forward presence of U.S. military forces. We have exerted this presence
through forces permanently stationed abroad;
through a network of bases, facilities, and logistics arrangements; and through the operational
presence provided by periodic patrols, exercises,
and visits of U.S. military units. Clearly, the mix

of these elements will change as our perception of the threat changes, as technology improves the capabilities and reach of our military forces, and as allies assume greater responsibilities in our common efforts. But our forward presence will remain a critical part of our defense posture for the foreseeable future. Our overseas bases serve as an integral part of our alliances and foster co-operation against common threats. There is no better assurance of a U.S. security commitment than the presence of U.S. forces.

There are growing pressures for change in our global deployments, however. Some are caused by concerns at home over an inequitable sharing of the defense burden, and others in host countries emanate from nationalism, anti-nuclear sentiment, environmental and social concerns and honestly divergent interests. Operational restrictions on our forces overseas are also increasing, some of which we can accommodate with new training and technologies, but others of which may eventually reduce the readiness of our deployed units.

In Europe, the overall level and specific contribution of U.S. forces are not etched in stone, but we will maintain forces in Europe—ground, sea and air, conventional and nuclear—for as long as they are needed and wanted, as I have pledged. Our forces in Europe contribute in many ways to stability and security. They are not tied exclusively to the size of the Soviet presence in Eastern Europe, but to the overall Alliance response to the needs of security. For the foreseeable future, we believe a level of 195,000 U.S. troops in Central Europe is appropriate for maintaining stability after a CFE reduction.

We also recognize that the presence of our forces creates burdens that are part of the overall sharing of effort within the Alliance. Consistent with the demands of readiness, we will work to adjust our training and other activities to ease the burden they impose.

Outside of Europe, we will maintain the ability to respond to regional crises, to support our commitments, and to pursue our security interests. Within that policy, adjustments in our overseas presence will be made. Yet—even as the total number of U.S. forward-deployed forces is reduced—we will work to preserve a U.S. presence where needed. And, where appropriate, we will work to ensure continued access to facilities that will permit a prompt return of U.S. forces should they be required. As we negotiate for the use of overseas bases, we will also proceed from the realistic premise that no base is irreplaceable. While some are preferred more than others, each makes a limited contribution to our strategy.

Sharing the Responsibilities of Collective Defense

The success of our postwar strategy has enabled allied and friendly nations' economies and societies to flourish. We now look to them to assume a greater share in providing for our common security. Our efforts in this regard will be integrated with our plans for future force structure, weapons modernization, and arms control. Above all, they must not be—nor be perceived to be—a cover for "burden shedding".

Our deliberations will be less about different ways to calculate defense burdens and more about increasing overall capabilities. One promising approach is a greater commitment to national specialization, an improved intra-alliance division of labor based on the comparative advantages of different allies in different defense activities. Such an approach could reduce the impact of budget constraints being felt by us all. Significant adjustments in missions and national force structures may be possible as part of major negotiated force reductions, such as those envisioned by CFE. The overall destruction of equipment and the possibility of "cascading" newer items from one Alliance member to another (while destroying older, less capable models) may give us opportunities for greater efficiencies and new forms of Alliance cooperation. These are complex issues, however, and any steps will have to be sensitive to issues of national sovereignty and based on an Alliance-wide consensus.

As a part of burdensharing, the United States will continue to ask our economically stronger allies to increase aid to other Alliance members and to friendly Third World countries. As another element of burdensharing, the United

States will work with allies to broaden the regional role of our forward-deployed forces. This will help us deal with the challenge of maintaining sufficient forces for local defense and the forces for likely contingencies elsewhere—a challenge that will grow as defense resources become more constrained. In support of this objective, we will make forward-deployed forces more mobile and flexible so they can assume broader regional responsibilities in addition to deterring attack in the country in which they are located.

Forces for the Third World

Since World War II, the threat posed by the Soviet Union has dominated much of our planning for the Third World. But we have also worked to preserve peace and build democracy and we have long identified specific interests independent of a Soviet factor. In the future, we expect that non-Soviet threats to these interests will command even greater attention.

To the degree possible, we will support allied and friendly efforts rather than introduce U.S.

forces. Nonetheless, we must retain the capability to act either in concert with our allies or, if necessary, unilaterally where our vital interests are threatened.

The growing technological sophistication of Third World conflicts will place serious demands on our forces. They must be able to respond quickly, and appropriately, as the application of even small amounts of power early in a crisis usually pays significant dividends. Some actions may require considerable staying power, but there are likely to be situations where American forces will have to succeed rapidly and with a minimum of casualties. Forces will have to accommodate to the austere environment, immature basing structure, and significant ranges often encountered in the Third World. The logistics "tail" of deployed forces will also have to be kept to a minimum, as an overly large American presence could be self-defeating. These capabilities will sometimes be different from those of a force optimized for a conflict in Europe, and—as our understanding of the threat there evolves—we will make the necessary adjustments.

We will also try to involve other industrial democracies in preventing and resolving Third World conflicts. Some of our Atlantic allies have strong political, economic, cultural, and military ties with Third World countries, and Japan provides considerable sums of aid. Their role will become even more important in the future.

The Mobilization Base

The United States has never maintained active forces in peacetime adequate for all the possible contingencies we could face in war. We have instead relied on reserve forces and on a pool of manpower and industrial strength that we could mobilize to deal with emergencies beyond the capabilities of our active units.

For almost two decades, our Total Force policy has placed a significant portion of our total military power in a well-equipped, well-trained, and early-mobilizing reserve component. Various elements of that policy—the balance between active and reserve forces, the mix of units in the two components, the nature of missions given reserve forces—are likely to be adjusted as we respond to changes in the security environment. Reserve forces are generally less expensive to maintain than their active counterparts so, as we adjust force structures, retaining reserve units is one alternative for reducing costs while still hedging against uncertainties. It is an alternative we must thoroughly explore, especially as we better understand the amount of warning time we can expect for a major conflict.

A credible industrial mobilization capability contributes to deterrence and alliance solidarity by demonstrating to adversaries and friends alike that we are able to meet our commitments. While important progress has been made in recent years, more can be done to preserve our ability to produce the weapons and equipment we need. Mobilization plans will also have to reflect our changing understanding of warning for a global war and develop graduated responses that will themselves signal U.S. resolve and thus contribute to deterrence.

Chemical Warfare

Our primary goal is to achieve an effective, truly global ban on chemical weapons as soon as possible. Until such a ban is achieved, the United States will retain a small but effective chemical weapons stockpile to deter the use of chemical weapons against us and our allies. We will also continue our initiatives to protect our forces from chemical agents that could be used against them and to minimize the impact of being forced to operate in a chemical environment.

We will never use chemical weapons first, but only in retaliation for their use against us. For as long as we retain a chemical weapons deterrent, we will ensure that it is as safe and effective as possible.

Space

The United States remains committed to the exploration and use of space for peaceful purposes and the benefit of all mankind, but international law and this commitment allow for activities to protect our national security. Our objectives for space mirror those which we have long held for the sea—to ensure free access for all in time of peace, but to be able to deny access to our enemies in time of war.

Our space activities will help deter and, if necessary, defend against enemy attack. We will maintain assured access to space and negate, if necessary, hostile space systems. We will develop, acquire, and deploy systems for communications, navigation, environmental monitoring, early warning, surveillance, and treaty verification.

We will also pursue scientific, technological, and economic benefit—including encouraging private sector investment. We will promote international cooperative activities and work with others to maintain freedom in space.

We remain dedicated to expanding human presence and activity beyond earth orbit and into the solar system. In July I committed the United States to return to the moon, this time to stay, and continue with a journey to Mars. The first step in this bold program to strengthen our position of space leadership will be completion of Space Station Freedom in the 1990s.

I chartered the National Space Council, chaired by Vice President Quayle, to develop national space policy, advise me on space matters, and ensure that policy guidance is carried out. I have also asked the Vice President, as Chairman of the Council, to assess the feasibility of international cooperation in human exploration. Equally important, I announced our commitment to use space to address critical environmental problems on earth. The new Mission to Planet Earth program, a major part of a comprehensive research effort, will use space platforms to gather the data we need to determine what changes are taking place in the global environment.

The National Space Council also provides a high-level focus for commercial space issues. Consistent with national security and safety, an expanding private sector role in space can generate economic benefits for the nation.

Low-Intensity Conflict

Even as the threat of East-West conflict may be diminishing in a new era, lower-order threats like terrorism, subversion, insurgency, and drug trafficking are menacing the United States, its citizenry, and its interests in new ways.

Low-intensity conflict involves the struggle of competing principles and ideologies below the level of conventional war. Poverty and the lack of political freedoms contribute to the instability that breeds such conflict. Our response must address these underlying conditions—but we cannot accept violence against our interests, or even less against innocent civilians, as a legitimate instrument of anyone's policy. Nor can the ideals of democracy, freedom, or economic progress be nurtured except in an environment of security.

It is the primary responsibility of friendly nations to protect their own interests. Our security assistance programs are a crucial tool with which we can help them help themselves. In some cases, security assistance ought to assume the same priority as resources devoted to our own forces.

It is not possible to prevent or deter conflict at the lower end of the conflict spectrum in the same way or to the same degree as at the higher. American forces therefore must be capable of dealing effectively with the full range of threats, including insurgency and terrorism. Special Operations Forces have particular utility in this environment, but we will also pursue new and imaginative ways to apply flexible general purpose forces to these problems. We will improve the foreign language skills and cultural orientation of our armed forces and adjust our intelligence activities to better serve our needs. Units with unique capabilities in this environment will receive increased emphasis. Training and research and development will be better attuned to the needs of low-intensity conflict.

Drug Trafficking

The Department of Defense, as noted earlier, has an important role to play in our National Drug

Control Strategy in coordination with the Department of State and law enforcement agencies.

The first line of defense against the illegal flow
of drugs is at the source—in those countries
where illicit drugs are produced and processed
before being sent to the United States and other
countries. Our policy is to strengthen the political
will and institutional capability of host-country
military, judicial, and law enforcement agencies.
Training and material assistance help improve
tactical intelligence and the ability to conduct air-
mobile and riverine operations. Security assistance also provides host countries with the
resources needed to confront the insurgency
threats that often are endemic to narcotics-
producing regions.

A second line of defense involves the deployment of appropriate elements of the U.S. Armed
Forces with the primary role of detecting and
monitoring the transportation of drugs to the
U.S. border. The Secretary of Defense has directed several regional commanders to support
these objectives with their own programs and op-

erations. As a high priority, our military counter-narcotics deployments will focus on the flow of drugs—especially cocaine—across the Caribbean, Central America, and Mexico toward the southern border of the United States. These deployments will support U.S. law enforcement agencies in their efforts to apprehend traffickers and seize drug shipments.

Our military and foreign intelligence activities must be coordinated with our own and host-country law enforcement agencies to identify air and maritime smuggling vessels as well as the networks that facilitate and manage illicit drug trafficking. This cooperation and coordination must be extended to the operational level to ensure timely and effective interdiction.

Current efforts are already bearing fruit. Our assistance to the Colombian government has aided its courageous campaign to strike back at the drug lords and to reestablish national sovereignty and the rule of law. The cocaine industry in the Andean region has been disrupted, and sustained pressure and cooperation will erode the strength of the drug trafficking organizations. The United States is committed to such a sustained international effort.

Intelligence Programs

The extraordinary changes taking place in the world are posing an almost unprecedented challenge to our intelligence assets and programs.

The changes in East-West relations point to a more peaceful future. But—after four decades of confrontation—achieving mutual trust will be a difficult task of confidence-building and verification. A time of transition can also be a time of turbulence. It will be critical that we be well informed of events and intentions in the Soviet Union, Eastern Europe, and elsewhere.

In a new period, intelligence must also focus on new issues. Within the Communist world, for example, economic questions take on new importance. As economic forces are the impetus for many of the military and political changes taking place there, economic change can be a valuable gauge of how much real change is occurring. The extent to which Soviet leaders actually shift resources from military to civilian uses, for example, will be an important strategic indicator.

In contrast to the hopeful trends in the Soviet Union and Eastern Europe, there are danger signs elsewhere—as this Report has noted. The proliferation of nuclear, chemical, and other military technologies raises the risks of conflict and crisis. Regional conflicts continue to fester. U.S. intelligence must monitor such developments and provide policymakers with the information needed to protect American interests.

The twin scourges of international terrorism and narcotics trafficking also pose very high-priority, but non-traditional, intelligence requirements. We will also have to adapt to a new emphasis on broader global economic and trade issues. We must be more fully aware of such subjects as foreign trade policies, economic trends, and foreign debt.

U.S. counterintelligence must be responsive to a changing hostile intelligence threat. Historically, foreign governments—and to some extent

foreign businesses—have tried to obtain our se-
crets and technologies. Hostile intelligence efforts
are not likely to decrease in the near term, and
they may actually increase as barriers to contact
come down.

U.S. intelligence must still be the "alarm bell"
to give us early warning of new developments
and new dangers even as requirements grow in
number and complexity. Our intelligence capabilities must be ready to meet new challenges, to
adapt as necessary, and to support U.S. policy
in the 1990s.

Planning for the Future

United States military planning in the postwar
era has been dominated by the need to deter and
be able to defend against overwhelming Warsaw
Pact conventional forces in Europe. As this Report has described, this heretofore dominant real-
ity is undergoing significant change, both through
Soviet and other Warsaw Pact unilateral reductions and through negotiated agreements. This

prospect is clearly affecting our military planning.

Such planning need not and cannot await the entry into force of arms reduction treaties. We will not act merely on the promise of change in Warsaw Pact forces, but neither will we delay developing our responses to those changes until their implementation is upon us. We will continually review important issues like the future demands of nuclear deterrence, the proper role and mix of our general purpose forces, and an improved and more effective security assistance program.

·VII·

A PUBLIC TRUST

As our defense efforts adapt to changing circumstances, our people must be confident that their defense dollars are efficiently and effectively supporting the cause of peace.

The Defense Management Review

Shortly after I took office, I ordered a review of defense management structures and practices in order to improve defense acquisition, to implement the excellent recommendations of the Packard Commission, and to manage Department of Defense resources more effectively. Secretary Cheney completed a preliminary report and forwarded it to me in July, along with a commitment to implement its findings. I subsequently forwarded the report to the Congressional leadership, giving its recommendations my strong personal endorsement and asking for Congressional support in implementation.

The implementation process now underway provides for continuous improvement in several areas of defense management.

Reducing Overhead Costs While Maintaining Military Strength

The Department of Defense is building a significantly more streamlined acquisition structure with clear lines of responsibility and authority. The Services' systems and materiel commands are being reorganized to focus largely on logistics and support services. Nearly all contract administration services, currently divided among the Military Departments and the Defense Logistics Agency (DLA), are being consolidated under DLA. In addition, a Corporate Information Management initiative is underway to develop more efficient data processing and information systems.

Enhancing Program Performance

The Under Secretary of Defense for Acquisition will have an enhanced role and will discipline programs through a revised and strengthened acquisition process. Programs will have to achieve defined milestones and satisfy specific criteria before moving to the next phase of their development. The military departments will create a corps of officers who will make acquisition a full-time career. These and additional steps will lead to a simplified acquisition structure, run by well-trained, dedicated professionals able to perform their work with a minimum of bureaucratic distraction.

Reinvigorating Planning and Budgeting

The Secretary of Defense now chairs a new Executive Committee to review overall Department policies and permit regular and confidential exchanges on key issues among the Department's senior leadership. In addition, the Deputy Secretary manages a revitalized planning, programming, and budgeting system as Chairman of the Defense Planning and Resources Board. With steps such as these, the senior leadership in the Department is now engaged in a dynamic planning process that will improve the linkage between policy, strategy, programs, and budgets.

Reducing Micromanagement

The Department of Defense has begun to carve away a bewildering maze of self-imposed regulations. A new, streamlined set of directives will be issued this summer in a form that permits action at the working level, with little additional policy guidance. The Secretary of Defense, with my full indorsement, has called on Congress to work with the Administration to review and overhaul the statutory framework for defense acquisition and improve the process by which Congress oversees the Department.

Strengthening the Defense Industrial Base

The defense industrial base must be strong, and include manufacturers that are highly flexible and technologically advanced. This will require that both the Defense Department and industry maintain active research programs in vital technologies. The Department must also create incentives (and eliminate disincentives) to invest in new facilities and equipment as well as in research and development. This will be especially important in an era when overall procurements are likely to decline.

Improving the Observance of Ethical Standards

Secretary Cheney has chartered a high-level Ethics Council to develop ethics programs for the Department. The Council has met and directed work on a model ethics program, a Department-wide Ethics Conference, and a review of existing compliance programs. The goal is to strengthen ethical standards within government and with industry and to create an environment where official standards of conduct are well understood, broadly observed, and vigorously enforced.

The strength of this effort to improve defense management is that it is largely a product of the Department itself, not something forced on it from outside. The dedicated people—both civilian and military—who have developed the changes described above will be the same people called upon to make these changes work. These are not quick fixes but fundamental shifts, "cultural" changes, that address issues at the core of defense management. While we are proud of the accomplishments to date, fully achieving these ambitious objectives will require several years of significant effort.

Congress and the American People

Under our Constitution, responsibility for national defense is shared between the executive and legislative branches of our federal government. The President, for example, is commander-in-chief, while Congress has the power to raise and support armies and declare war. This system of shared and separated powers is well designed to guard against abuses of power, but it works best in the demanding environment of national security affairs only if there is a spirit of cooperation between the two branches and, indeed, a strong measure of national and bipartisan consensus on basic policy.

I am proud of the successful examples of bipartisan cooperation in the past year—on Central America, on aid to Eastern Europe, on Panama, to name a few. Yet other issues remain contentious, such as various attempts to constrict Presidential discretion and authority in fields ranging from covert actions to the excessive earmarking of assistance funds. If we are to make a successful transition to a new era, we need to work together.

We are now in an era of rapidly changing strategic conditions, new openings for peace, continuing uncertainties, and new varieties of danger. We thus face new opportunities and new problems, both of which demand of us special qualities of leadership—boldness, vision, and constancy. It is my responsibility to meet that challenge, and I am prepared to meet it in a spirit of close cooperation and consultation with Congress. I believe there is a national consensus in support of a strong foreign and defense policy—perhaps broader and deeper than at any time in 25 years. Congress and the President need, more than ever, to reflect that unity in their own cooperation. We owe the American people no less.